BOOK ENDORSEMENTS

Ophelia's book is a fabulous blend of science and faith. At a time when forces seek to divide us, it is wonderfully refreshing to see common ground for any who loves science and study and at the same time hold deeply held religious beliefs. I love the daily devotional format of her book, with a scientific story/truism, a spiritual story compliment, and a hope and prayer for understanding and strength. Well done, Ophelia!

Stephen Portz
Albert Einstein Distinguished Educator
Author, *Teaching the New Millennium Problem Solvers, SySTEMic Ed Blog.*

"Seeing God through STEM" is an inspirational collection of articles and stories that demonstrate how God's amazing creations show of His infinite love for us. Ophelia Barizo, who has spent her entire career as a STEM educator, shares her personal reflections and thoughts in language that children can relate to and understand. Her love for the Master Creator and her desire to minister to children are evident in this lovely collection of STEM worship thoughts. This is an excellent resource for parents and teachers alike.

Janesta Walker
Superintendent of Education
Chesapeake Conference of Seventh-day Adventists

Rarely do you find an author who can knit together the amazing things of science with a personal understanding of the things of God. Not only is Ophelia Barizo a wonderful teacher and scientist, but she has also spent her life journeying and discussing her findings with the One who created it all. Those who read this book will not only come away with more knowledge about the world of STEM but will also gain glimpses into another world where an awesome God never runs out of astounding ideas!

Kandace Zollman
Pastor of Nurture
Spencerville Adventist Church

SEEING GOD THROUGH
STEM

OPHELIA M. BARIZO

WESTBOW
PRESS®
A DIVISION OF THOMAS NELSON
& ZONDERVAN

This book is a work of non-fiction. Unless otherwise noted, the author and the publisher make no explicit guarantees as to the accuracy of the information contained in this book and in some cases, names of people and places have been altered to protect their privacy.

WestBow Press books may be ordered through booksellers or by contacting:

WestBow Press
A Division of Thomas Nelson & Zondervan
1663 Liberty Drive
Bloomington, IN 47403
www.westbowpress.com
844-714-3454

Because of the dynamic nature of the Internet, any web addresses or links contained in this book may have changed since publication and may no longer be valid. The views expressed in this work are solely those of the author and do not necessarily reflect the views of the publisher, and the publisher hereby disclaims any responsibility for them.

Any people depicted in stock imagery provided by Getty Images are models, and such images are being used for illustrative purposes only. Certain stock imagery © Getty Images.

All scripture quotations are taken from The Holy Bible, New International Version®, NIV® Copyright © 1973, 1978, 1984, 2011 by Biblica, Inc.® Used by permission. All rights reserved worldwide.

ISBN: 979-8-3850-0280-1 (sc)
ISBN: 979-8-3850-0281-8 (e)

Library of Congress Control Number: 2023913135

Print information available on the last page.

WestBow Press rev. date: 09/13/2023

CONTENTS

DEDICATION

In Memoriam: To Salvador and Bienvenida Miraflores, who instilled in me early in life, the love of God and the love of nature.

> This book is dedicated to my grandchildren, Ada Emmelina and Orion James. May you never lose the sense of wonder and curiosity about nature and this world and continue to appreciate and love Creation and the Creator.

PREFACE

As a high school science teacher in a Christian school for many years I tried to integrate faith and learning in as many scientific concepts as possible. I was inspired by my physics teacher Miss Ester Manalaysay, whom we affectionately called Miss Man. Miss Man also happened to be my dad's physics teacher. Miss Man was a quintessential science teacher. Her hair was meticulously arranged in a bun behind her head, her spectacles resting comfortably on her nose. Although her class was one of the few classes I did not get an A in, which bothered me quite a bit, I was really impressed by her spiritual lesson for every law in physics. I wrote down every spiritual lesson in my notebook, but after several moves, one across the Pacific Ocean and three more in North America, that precious notebook got lost in transition.

My father was also an early inspiration. He was never my teacher in the classroom, but he taught me by example. I remember trips to shallow tide pools where we would observe the colorful fish, sea stars, sea anemones, jellyfish, and other marine creatures. We were never allowed to take them out of their natural environment. I remember days when we would be catching insects with nets and with our hands for one of his school projects. I remember walks on the beach and Saturday afternoon nature walks.

In 2013-2014 I served as an Albert Einstein Distinguished Educator Fellow at the National Science Foundation. There I learned more about STEM: science, technology, engineering, and mathematics. After that fellowship year, I started to teach STEM classes and started a STEM program at my school.

The idea of integrating STEM with spiritual things in worship talks came during the lowest point of my life when I was diagnosed with sarcoma on my leg. After undergoing two surgeries to remove the tumors and several sessions of proton radiation therapy, I am now free of the disease, thanks to God's marvelous healing power and the prayers of so many loved ones, colleagues, and friends. During this difficult time, God gave me the idea of preparing and presenting STEM worships to students and to write a book when I had more time to do so. For the last three years, I have been giving STEM-focused worship talks to students in several states and in the Philippines. I retired in June 2022, giving me some time to write in between trips to faraway places with my husband. I firmly believe that STEM helps us to appreciate and understand God's Creation more. It is my desire that these short devotionals, which integrate faith and learning with STEM, will draw students closer to our Creator, who is the ultimate source of wisdom.

FOREWORD

Greetings,

With immense pleasure I write this foreword for the remarkable book, *Seeing God Through STEM*. As a physician-scientist who witnesses the awe-inspiring integration of science and faith daily, I am delighted to see a devotional book specifically designed to inspire and guide young minds in the world of STEM.

Throughout history, humanity has been fascinated by the natural world's mysteries, and science has provided us with tools to unlock some of those mysteries. As a physician, I have witnessed firsthand the incredible advancements in medical technology, the marvels of biological systems, and the intricate balance of nature. In this context, *Seeing God Through STEM* holds great significance.

Integrating faith and science is not only possible, but it is also necessary for a well-rounded understanding of our existence. This book beautifully captures the essence of this integration by inviting readers to explore the wonders of science, technology, engineering, and mathematics through a lens of faith. It serves as a guiding light for young individuals seeking to harmonize their spiritual beliefs with their passion for the STEM fields, and reminds us that science, at its core, is a process of discovery that reveals the intricacies of the Creator's handiwork.

It is my hope that *Seeing God Through STEM* serves as an inspiration for young minds, empowering them to pursue excellence in their scientific endeavors while deepening their faith. May this book inspire a new generation of scientists, engineers, and thinkers who approach their work with reverence and a profound appreciation for the wonders of creation.

With great admiration for the author and enthusiasm for the impact this book will have,
James Gulley, MD, Ph.D. F.A.C.P.
National Cancer Institute, Bethesda, Maryland

ACKNOWLEDGEMENT

Several people have made this writing project possible. I would like to show them my sincere gratitude.

- Daniel Barizo, my husband, continues to be my biggest steadfast support, my best friend, my loving partner, my travel buddy, and my biggest fan. I thank God for him and his love for me, which has given me so much happiness, and strength during trying times.
- My children, Jennifer, and Amanda, for their love, care, and for being there for me in good times and difficult times. They are my pride and joy.
- Wolfram Koessel and Elizabeth Lanning for their love and support, and for all my prayer partners who have shown me love by praying with and for me.
- Colleagues and friends who read portions of the book and for their input – Barbie Buckner, Colleen Lay, Arnie Nielsen, Stephen Portz, Janesta Walker, and Kandace Zollman.
- Megan Mason for proofreading the final draft of this book.
- My students over the last 43 years of my teaching. You have encouraged me and inspired me to be the best teacher that I could be. I love all of you. You will always be "my kids."

DEVOTIONALS

LEARNING FROM NATURE

Job 12:7-10 - "But ask the animals, and they will teach you, or the birds in the sky, and they will tell you, or speak to the earth, and it will teach you, or let the fish in the sea inform you. Which of all these does not know that the hand of the Lord has done this? In his hand is the life of every creature and the breath of all humankind."

Did you know that scientists, engineers, and inventors learn incredible amounts of information and ideas from nature? Nature is the inspiration behind many gadgets and inventions that are important, necessary, and even lifesaving. Biomimicry is the science of using inspiration from nature and nature's designs to create inventions to solve human problems. We copy, or mimic, designs from nature and use them as models for inventing new products.

Plants have ways of scattering their seeds to produce new generations of plants. One day George de Mestral went for a walk with his dog. When he got back from his walk, he found burrs of burdock thistles clinging to his clothing and his dog's fur. He examined the burrs under the microscope and discovered tiny hooks at the end of the burrs that allowed the seeds to attach themselves to animals and people's clothes to help them spread. For ten years, he worked to develop a special fabric called Velcro, used in fastening things together. You will find Velcro in shoes and clothing, blood pressure gauges, hanging artwork, patient gowns, diapers, classrooms, space travel to prevent small objects from floating away in zero gravity, and a whole host of other things. Can you think of other ways where you can use Velcro?

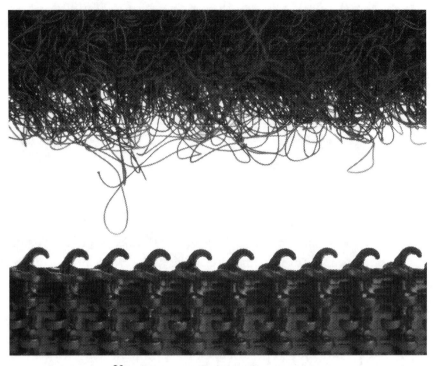

VELCRO – HOOK AND LOOP FASTENER

Have you seen insects get stuck in a spider's web? How do spiders get to their food without getting stuck? When a spider spins its web, it makes only certain lines sticky. Of course, the spider itself knows which ones are sticky and which ones are not, so it navigates on the non-sticky lines to get to its prey! Have you ever had a bandage pulled off your skin that really hurt and made marks on your skin? Scientists, looking to the spider's web for inspiration, are designing a special medical tape that comes off without damaging the sensitive skin of infants and older patients. The tape has three layers. A laser etches a grid on the sticky layer, leaving non-sticky parts. This tape, when removed, will come off without pain or damage to sensitive skin.

Nature has a way of solving our problems, but we know who can solve all our problems. Although, we know that Jesus is the answer to all our problems, we need to exercise faith and trust to discover what His will is for us. Isaiah 65:24 says, "Before they call I will answer;

while they are still speaking, I will hear." Let us trust God with all our problems because He has the solutions.

Dear Jesus, help me to trust God in every aspect of my life, since I know He has all the answers and solutions to any problem I face.

BARBIE IN SPACE!

Matthew 24:42 - "Therefore keep watch, because you do not know on what day your Lord will come."

Most girls have played with Barbie dolls at some time in their lives. I never did – my parents were too poor to buy me the dolls. My first toy was a stuffed Koala bear whose nose and arms kept falling off after a while, although my mother painstakingly sewed them on countless times. Barbie has been a child's toy for more than sixty years, having been launched as a toy in 1959. Girls still enjoy playing with Barbie dolls, and there are even TV shows and movies featuring Barbie.

Barbie has now launched into space! Barbie been dressed for space for the past 60 years, but now her dream has come true! Two Barbies are now on board the International Space Station (ISS). The International Space Station is the largest space station in earth's orbit. Astronauts travel to the space station in space shuttles and stay there for several months before the shuttle returns with their replacements and brings them back to earth. Astronauts who live in the space station do all sorts of scientific projects and experiments, including the effects of space travel on the human body.

Bringing Barbie dolls into space is part of "Mission DreamStar," a project to inspire girls to go into STEM (Science, Technology, Engineering, and Mathematics) careers. The dolls have been in orbit since February 2022. The dolls have been dressed like Sally Ride, the first American woman in space, and Anna Kikina, a Russian cosmonaut.

Mattel, the toy company that manufactures Barbie, has sent another Barbie astronaut resembling astronaut Samantha Cristoforetti to the ISS recently. This Barbie aims to encourage and kindle girls' passion "to become the next generation of astronauts, engineers, and space scientists." These Barbie dolls are also for sale to aspiring girl astronauts to inspire their enthusiasm for STEM.

A Barbie doll dressed as an astronaut.

What kindles your passion? Are you enthusiastic about Christ's second coming, and going with Him to heaven? When we are in heaven and on the New Earth, we will be exploring faraway galaxies in the universe. We won't be stuck in a space station, where we must wait for a space shuttle to take us back to earth. I can hardly wait to have these awesome field trips with Jesus, our Master Teacher and the Creator of the Universe! Will we be traveling at the speed of light or the speed of thought? It really does not matter since we will have all eternity to explore! I am so excited just thinking about it.

Dear Jesus, help me to be passionate for You and enthusiastically prepare for Your coming. There is no other way that would be more exciting than spending eternity with You!

BEE ENGINEERING

Proverbs 24:13,14 - "Eat honey, my son, for it is good, honey from the comb is sweet to your taste. Know also that wisdom is sweet to your soul; if you find it, there is a future hope for you, and your hope will not be cut off."

I was just getting into a friend's pool when a hornet hovering close by dove in and stung me on my palm. Out comes the EpiPen, and a stab on the thigh hopefully takes care of it. Luckily, my friend, a doctor, was at the poolside and treated me, so I did not have to go to the ER. I'm allergic to bees, wasps, and yellow jackets, but I am the only one getting stung in the family – Murphy's law. I must stay away from these pesky insects, but the love of the great outdoors makes me take the risk every time! Despite this fear of getting stung, I really do like bees and am in awe of all the science, mathematics, and engineering that bees have in them to live their lives.

The construction of the honeycomb is fascinating, since it is constructed by worker honeybees less than 17 days old. The bees' knowledge of geometry is remarkable! These combs are all 5 mm wide and 11 mm deep, with walls 88 micrometers thick, which is about 1/350 of an inch! Each comb is a perfect hexagon, which is an exceptionally strong, flexible, and efficient shape. How do the young bees know this, and how do they know that the walls are so strong that one pound of the comb can carry twenty-five pounds of honey? Honeycombs are truly miracles of architecture and engineering!

BEES INSIDE THE BEEHIVE ON HEXAGONAL HONEYCOMBS

But wait a minute! Have you heard about the bees' waggle dance? This dance is a way of communicating to other bees the location of the field of flowers that will provide them with their most important food source. The number of times the bee waggles its abdomen and the angles of the dance on the vertical honeycomb stands for the distance to the flowers and the direction of the food source in relation to the sun. This relationship is not simple arithmetic but logarithmic. What is amazing is that bees can communicate this distance to humans, who by doing mathematical calculations can find the field of flowers!

If bees were humans, these are only some of the instruments they would need to do their jobs – rulers, protractors, vernier calipers, computers, light and wind sensors, compasses, navigational systems, complex internal circuitry, and many other instruments. How would these devices fit into the tiny body of a bee? Bees are so critically important - their very existence is vital to our lives, providing us with fruits and vegetables for healthy living and for life itself. Honey and bees are blessings that God has given us. Furthermore, bees are examples of hard work, cooperation, and wisdom. I am thankful for bees, but I can't wait for the time that bees will lose their sting!

Our Creator and King, thank You for creating the tiny yet mighty bees, which pollinate our plants so that we can enjoy wonderful fruits and vegetables for our health. Thank You that the mathematical and scientific complexity of the bees' jobs help us to appreciate Your creative power. Help us to learn wonderful, spiritual lessons from bees.

BIOBULLIES: ALIEN INVADERS

1 Corinthians 10:13 – "No temptation has seized you except what is common to man. And God is faithful, he will not let you be tempted beyond what you can bear. But when you are tempted, he will also provide a way out so that you can stand up under it."

What happens when plants and animals hitchhike on cars, ships, planes, or are brought into another biome either accidentally or on purpose? Since these organisms do not have natural enemies in their new homes, they may multiply rapidly and threaten the existence of plants and animals that normally live in their own biomes. These foreign invaders are called invasive alien species. Some alien species do not cause harm to the native species, but when they do, they take over natural habitats, cause environmental and economic damage, and in serious cases, the extinction of several native species. These alien species are sometimes called **biobullies** because they threaten the plants and animals in their natural environments.

The Burmese python, one of the largest snakes in the world, is an example of an alien species. Burmese pythons were introduced to Florida as exotic pets in the 1970s and 1980s. These giant snakes can grow up to 20 feet long and weigh more than 250 pounds. Some owners who were unable to manage them or find homes for them, released them into the wild. The pythons have been found to eat 70 different animals in the Everglades, even alligators. They also compete with other animals for food and homes.

BURMESE PYTHON

The kudzu vine is a creeping invasive plant that has taken over other plants in the Southern United States and is moving westward. It was introduced to the US from Japan during an expo in Philadelphia. It was also planted to control erosion, but its growth exploded. It grows at the rate of one foot per day, terrorizes other plants, and grows over anything in its path.

KUDZU TAKING OVER A FOREST.

The story of Joseph is an example of bullying in the Bible. Joseph's brothers were bullies. The fact that he had a coat of many colors from his father made them bully him more. They were cruel to him, threw him in a pit, left him for dead, and sold him to Arab traders. Joseph was eventually sold to the Egyptians. Bullying can happen anywhere – at school, at home, or even at the work. Satan is the ultimate bully, but Jesus will stand up to him for us and will defeat him.

Invasive alien species in nature is the result of sin. Sin is invasive. It can take residence in our heart and life and spread into our whole being. But sin does not have to threaten us, as invasive species threatens nature. God gives us the power to overcome sin.

Dear God, please infuse me with the Holy Spirit to give me the strength to resist temptation and remove sin from my life. Please banish away the invasiveness of sin that threatens me from receiving eternal life.

CARING IS SHARING

Matthew 22:36-39 - "'Teacher, which is the greatest commandment in the Law?" Jesus replied, "Love the Lord your God with all your heart and with all your soul and with all your mind. This is the first and greatest commandment. And the second is like it. "Love your neighbor as yourself." All the Law and the Prophets hang on these two commandments."'

COVID was an international pandemic, something the world never experienced before! We all are now too familiar with the fear of contracting the dreaded disease, the lockdowns, the isolation, the travel bans, and the anxiety of being with people, even the people we love.

However, there were some positive things about COVID. After not being able to see their loved ones for months, people learned to appreciate their families more. People started to value nature and the great outdoors, going on more hikes and walks in the woods, the beaches, and the parks, since those offered safe places away from crowds. People began to find creative ways of doing things. Mt. Everest was visible for miles because smog and pollution were greatly reduced. The pandemic changed the way we live in more ways than one-and we will never be the same.

Tembok Gede, a small village in Indonesia, developed a creative way of caring for and communicating with members of their community who contracted the contagious disease. The townspeople, led by Aseyanto (he only has one name), a leader in the neighborhood, developed a resourceful and innovative way of using trash to assemble a robot. They named the robot Delta, after the contagious COVID variant that ravished the village. The robot was made of simple materials, such as a car chassis, an old television, pots and pans, a rice cooker, and other discarded household materials. It was controlled remotely and had a battery life of 12 hours. Its task was to deliver disinfectants, food, good cheer, and comfort to quarantine shut ins. As it delivered its supplies it would utter "assalamu'alaikum" (Peace be with you), followed by, "A delivery is here. Get well soon."

A ROBOT IN INDONESIA REMINDING
PEOPLE TO WEAR THEIR MASKS.
PHOTO CREDIT: SHUTTERSTOCK

I am sure the people who had COVID appreciated the kind gestures of Aseyanto and his team of helpers. They helped carry their neighbors' burdens, gave them food, and served them their needs during a difficult time in their lives. Galatians 6:2 says, "Carry each other's burdens, and in this way, you fulfill the law of Christ." When you care for others you develop a sense of purpose, and this sense of purpose translates to feeling good about yourself. It also fosters closer connections with other people, but above all you are fulfilling a commandment of love, sharing God's love to those around you.

Dear Father, help me to be attentive to the needs of those around me, and try to aid in any way I can. I know that when I support others in need, I am making You, me, and other people happy. I am also sharing Your love and bringing people closer to You.

CHILD'S PLAY

Isaiah 11:6-8 – "The wolf will live with lamb, the leopard will lie down with the goat, the calf and the lion and the yearling together; and a little child will lead them. The cow will feed with the bear, their young will lie down together, and the lion will eat straw like the ox. The infant will play near the cobra's den, and the young child will put its hand into the viper's nest."

When I was young, my parents regularly took us outdoors to play. We had excursions to the beach, the zoo, and the park. We would run, play tag and hide-and-seek, pick flowers, and chase butterflies. My happiest memories were at the beach, where we would wade and splash in the shallows and pick shells, starfish, catch colorful fish, and watch colorful sea anemones swaying their tentacles.

Children were made to be active and explore through creative play. Active exploration, especially outdoors and in nature, helps children to develop physically, mentally, socially, and spiritually. Unfortunately, some children are born with or develop diseases so early in their lives. These conditions limit their ability to run and play like other kids. Other children may have serious accidents that prevent them from engaging in fun physical activities.

Young children between the age of one and three are too small to use wheelchairs currently on the market. Dr. Teresa Plummer, a professor of occupational therapy, recognized this need, and worked with a Permobil, a company that manufactures wheelchairs. She helped develop *The Explorer Mini*, a powered mobility device designed for children 1-3 years of age. It is the first and only one of its kind. The Invention was recognized as one of the top 100 inventions of 2021 by *Time* magazine.

The device allows children to move around and explore using a joystick. Since it increases mobility, it also helps the child develop in other areas. The device helps the children interact more with their environment. Children are having fun using the colorful modified wheelchair, thinking it is cool.

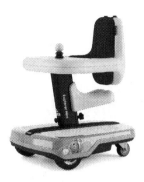

THE EXPLORER MINI
PHOTO CREDIT: PERMOBIL AMERICAS

Won't it be cool when all children can explore endlessly in the new earth? The Bible says that a little child will be playing with animals that were considered wild on this earth. There will be no more childhood diseases, accidents, or physical ailments that will prevent children from being children. I would love to be a child again and explore God's creation with the faith of a little child.

Dear Jesus, help me to have faith like a little child, to trust You like a child trusts his parent; for I know that it is this childlike faith that is "the greatest in the kingdom of heaven." (Matthew 18:1)

FINDING FAKES

Psalm 139:13, 14 - "For you created my inmost being, you knit me together in my mother's womb. I praise you because I am fearfully and wonderfully made; your works are wonderful."

Fabulous finds at an auction or yard sale are wonderful! The lucky one may score a real painting from the 17th century and make a handsome profit – and this happens occasionally. Many people collect art as a hobby or for investment. Many works of art can fetch thousands or even millions of dollars in auction. Forged art may include paintings, sculptures, and indigenous art. This interest in art has spawned an industry of art forgery, or fake artwork. Counterfeiters go through a lot of work to deceive unsuspecting collectors and make illegal profits. Fake art has resulted in the forfeiture of millions of dollars in revenue or personal loss.

How do you know the art you snagged at a thrift store or bought from an art dealer is real or fake? Science has developed ways of spotting counterfeit art. Usually; the first step is to trace the history of ownership of the painting or a paper trail of sale transactions. Documents of sale are examined, and a lot of research is done on how the painting was passed from one owner to another. One of the simplest ways is by examining the painting visually using a magnifying glass. Microscopes are also used to examine fibers and paints. X-ray fluorescence can determine the metal elements present in the painting, and ultraviolet and infrared analysis may detect repairs. Recently, a newer method of finding forgeries is digital analysis of the work of art. Science has emerged as a valuable tool in finding and detecting forged work as well as created a new breed of counterfeit busters with specialized training in these scientific techniques.

OIL PAINTING OF MONA LISA BY LEONARDO DA VINCI

Is there any such thing as counterfeit Christianity? How can someone be a Christian and be a counterfeit at the same time? The devil, the master of counterfeiters, is hard at work to bring us the counterfeit of truths. Do you work hard for your salvation? Do you say you are a Christian and not practice what you preach? Do spend so much time doing good things for Christ that you do not have time to develop a relationship with your Maker? Christianity is not a set rules or do's or don'ts. It is a relationship with our Creator, our Maker, our Father -- that includes spending special, unhurried time in communing with him in study and prayer every day. It is sharing His love to those around you by witnessing for Him and drawing people to Him. We are God's masterpiece. Let us allow God to perfect His masterpiece in the tapestry of our hearts and not allow the counterfeiter to mess with God's artwork.

Thank You, Jesus, for creating me in Your image. Infuse me with Your truths. Help me to allow You to restore me to Your image, a masterpiece of Your creation.

FROM TRASH TO MUSIC

2 Corinthians 5: 17 - Therefore, if anyone is in Christ, the new creation has come: The old has gone, the new is here!

MUSICAL INSTRUMENTS FROM TRASH
PHOTO CREDIT: SHUTTERSTOCK

Have you heard music played from instruments made from trash? There is an orchestra whose young members perform on instruments made from trash, performing music of Beethoven, Mozart, and even the Beatles. The orchestra produces pleasant vibrations from recycled trash!

The vibrations of an object produce sound. When the object vibrates, it sends waves that travel through the air. The sound waves reach your ear, are funneled through your ear canal, and hit your eardrum, which sends vibrations to the auditory nerve. Your brain receives the sound and interprets it. Music is sound produced by regular vibrations. In music, sound may be produced by vibrating reeds or strings, a column of air, or a stretched membrane.

Cateura, Paraguay, is home to the largest landfill in the country. About 2,500 families live on the landfill and make their living sorting and picking through all the trash for valuables that they can sell. The idea of making instruments from trash was the brainchild of Favio Chavez, an environmental consultant, and Nicolas Gomez, a garbage picker. Their workshop produced an array of musical instruments. A cello's body is made from an oil drum, saxophone keys are made of bottlecaps, used X-ray films formed drum set skins, and violins are fashioned out of cans and wooden spoons. Tuning pegs are made from wooden utensils or worn-out shoe heels.

Favio Chavez, who has some musical experience, started teaching music lessons and started the orchestra. The Recycled Orchestra has come a long way. Since their humble beginnings, they have traveled beyond their borders to Brazil, Columbia, the United States, and the great music halls of Europe. They have even performed alongside Metallica and Megadeth and before Pope Francis - big accomplishments for a small, recycled orchestra from the impoverished community of Cateura! A documentary, *Landfill Harmonic*, has been produced and has been played all over the world. Other trash orchestras have now spawned in several countries, a testament to the creativity of Favio Chavez and Nicolas Gomez.

CATEURA ORCHESTRA PLAYING
INSTRUMENTS FROM THE LANDFILL.
PHOTO CREDIT: SHUTTERSTOCK

We are buried in the trash can of sin. Jesus picks up each one of us from this trash and transforms us into a thing of beauty. Just as a pupa is transformed into a beautiful butterfly, our sinful selves will be transformed into something beautiful, a testimony of His redeeming love and His salvation. We will become new in Christ.

Dear Jesus, thank You for Your ultimate gift of salvation. Thank You for taking me out of the trash can of sin and transforming my life to Your likeness. Help me to accept Your gift of salvation so that I may be a new person, reflecting Your love to those around me.

GARBAGE GOBBLERS

1 Corinthians 6:19,20 – "Do you not know that your bodies are temples of the Holy Spirit, who is in you, whom you have received from God? You are not your own; you were bought with a price. Therefore, honor God with your bodies."

I am sure no one wants to sunbathe on a beach full of litter or go kayaking on a river with plastic bottles and trash floating by their kayak. We like unspoiled, white-sand beaches and pristine rivers. This world is drowning in disposable trash. Plastic bottles, packaging materials, and other types of plastic waste are clogging our waterways and destroying the beauty of our lands, oceans, rivers, and lakes.

There is the nifty machine, an engineering marvel in Maryland invented by John Kellett in 2008, that uses the power of nature to remove trash from the Baltimore Harbor before it goes into the Chesapeake Bay and ultimately to the Atlantic Ocean. The machine was constructed using engineering ingenuity and is very successful as an ocean clean-up device. It is called the Mr. Trash Wheel. It is run by energy from flowing water. When the water level is low, no problem! A pump gets water from the river and pours it over the trash wheel to get it turning. The wheel has a conveyor belt that picks up trash from the water and takes it to bins behind the contraption to be taken away by trucks to be burned.

MR. TRASH WHEEL
PHOTO CREDIT: WATERFRONT
PARTNERSHIP OF BALTIMORE

Since 2014, when Mr. Trash Wheel was invented, many more trash wheels have been installed in Maryland's waterways. The other wheels were named Professor Trash Wheel, Captain Trash Wheel, and Gwynnda the Good Wheel of the West. The family of Trash Wheels has already collected more than 2,300 tons of trash, which includes plastic bags, plastic bottles, foam containers, sports balls, cigarette butts, a guitar, and–would you believe it–a snake!

There is a lot of trash in this world–trash coming into your minds from movies, music, books, and the internet. Some types of food also put the trash into your bodies, resulting in disease, and sometimes even death.

Your body is the temple of the Holy Spirit. Whatever you put into your body affects your health and eventually your mind, the only way God communicates with you. God talks to you through your mind. When you have a healthy body, you also have a healthy mind. That healthy mind helps you to have healthy relationships with others and with God. Let us not put garbage into the temple of God.

Dear Jesus, help me to choose what to put in my body and mind so that I do not desecrate Your holy temple, which is in me.

IN PRAISE OF SLIME

1 Corinthians 12:28 – "And God has placed in the church first of all apostles, second prophets, third teachers, then miracles, then gifts of healing, of helping, of guidance, and of different kinds of tongues."

Have you ever made slime and Silly Putty at school or at home? Making slime was a craze a few years ago. Children, even adults, played with rainbow slime, glitter slime, butter slime, crunchy slime, magnetic slime, and cloud slime, among many others, for hours. Slime could be stretched, pulled, molded into several shapes, and bounced. It also had a calming effect to some children.

Slime is a polymer. Polymers are interesting and important substances. They are giant molecules with hundreds to thousands of repeating units called monomers. The monomers react chemically to form polymers. Manufactured or synthetic polymers are so common now that they are in almost everything we use, from fabrics, toys, garden equipment, medical devices, plumbing pipes, food storage containers, lenses, cables, tools, and car parts. The list goes on and on. Polymers are important for their strength, flexibility, hardness, durability, and versatility. You may recognize some of the common names of polymers - nylon, Teflon, Styrofoam, polyvinyl chloride, acrylic, and polyethylene. There are also other polymers known as plastics that can be damaging to our environment.

Nature has its share of polymers. Most of these polymers are important for healthy body metabolism. Natural polymers include carbohydrates, proteins, silk, cellulose, and DNA. These polymers are necessary for life. Starch, a carbohydrate we get from rice, pasta, and bread, is a polymer of a simple sugar called glucose. DNA (deoxyribonucleic acid), a complex molecule made of very long chains, contains the instructions every living organism needs to make proteins, to reproduce, and to survive. It is also known as the "code of life."

THE DNA MOLECULE, A NATURAL POLYMER

The study of polymers reminds me that God has given each one of us many talents, just like polymers have literally hundreds of uses. These talents are also called spiritual gifts. Find out what you enjoy the most that can also help and bless other people. Do your best to improve your talent so that you can be more useful. Pray and ask God how you can best use your talent to witness for Him and to bring joy to others. If you play a musical instrument, find ways how you can make people happy with your talent. We can glorify God with the talents that He has given us.

Dear Jesus, thank You for my talents. Help me to discover and develop the talents You have given me and use them to bring service and joy to those around me. Help me to realize that if I do not use my talents I can lose them, and that would be a waste of the talents that could be used for the good of others and for Your glory.

GETTING LOST

Jeremiah 8:7 – "Even the stork in the sky knows her appointed seasons, and the dove, the swift and the thrush observe the time of their migration. But my people do not know the requirements of the Lord."

Have you ever gotten lost on a road trip? My family and I have, several times. When our children were young, we drove from Hamilton, Ontario to Vancouver across Canada on the way there and across the USA on the way back. We used maps and trip guides from AAA back then. We poured over maps and marked our route on a large map of North America.

Ancient people used constellations and stars to find their way. The Magi followed the Star as they searched for the Christ Child. The Star guided them to the greatest find of their lives. Today we have GPS (global positioning system), but we do get lost sometimes in cities where skyscrapers block the signals, and our GPS keeps "recalculating."

How does the GPS work? There are about 30 navigation satellites orbiting the earth at about 12,500 miles above earth. These satellites send signals to receivers on earth. Cell phones and hand-held GPS have these receivers. If they receive signals from at least four satellites, the receivers can calculate their exact positions. These calculations also help the GPS navigate and show us where we want to go.

A DRIVER USING GPS NAVIGATION ON A MOBILE PHONE

In life, sometimes we lose our way, not only geographically, but figuratively as well. We get confused and befuddled by certain decisions we must make. And then we worry if we are making the right decisions. William Cullen Bryant, an American poet, wrote: "He, who, from zone to zone, guides through the boundless sky thy certain flight, in the long way that I must trace alone, will lead my steps aright."

Canada geese migrate from north to south in the fall and back in the spring. Hummingbirds, as small as they are, migrate across the Gulf of Mexico. These birds do not lose their way. If God guides the paths of birds in their flights, even from one continent to another, we can trust that He will lead us in our lives.

Dear Lord, help me to trust God to lead me in all my decisions in life, big or small. I know that He directs the birds in their flights, and I trust that He will guide and direct my paths.

HAVE WINGLETS, WILL SOAR!

Genesis 1:21 – "So God created the great creatures of the sea and every living and moving thing with which the water teems, according to their kinds, and every winged bird according to its kind. And God saw that it was good."

One of my close friends who works for NASA and travels around the country often shows pictures of winglets on her social media posts. That got me curious about what was such a big deal about winglets, so I did some reading up on it. I also made it a point to look for winglets on my next flight. Sure enough, the wing of my plane had curved vertical wing extensions that pointed to the sky.

The idea of winglets was a brainchild of NASA engineer Richard Whitcomb, who was inspired by how birds curl up the ends of their wings as they soar in flight. Winglet, which means "little wing," was the name Whitcomb gave to vertical wing-shaped extensions at the end of airplane wings. He tested these winglets in a wind tunnel and found out that they reduced airplane drag. Drag is a combination of forces that slow down the movement of an airplane through the air.

AN AIRPLANE WINGLET

Later tests by a private company resulted in more modified and streamlined winglets that obtained greater efficiency in flight. Winglets are now used in most airlines and have resulted in savings of billions of dollars in fuel. The fuel efficiency, due to reduced drag, has also reduced carbon dioxide emissions from airplanes to 900 tons per aircraft each year. Since carbon dioxide is a greenhouse gas, this will make a difference in global warming. Anything that reduces pollution from the burning of fuel is a wonderful thing!

Interestingly, Whitcomb got his inspiration from birds. Nature has given scientists and engineers ideas on how to solve many of the world's problems or improve the existing designs of fabricated inventions. In this case, the problem of drag was reduced by a design from birds' wings. Nature truly has myriads of evidences of a Master Designer, who in His knowledge knew exactly how to create birds for flight. It is nice to know that we have a Creator who is so interested in birds' flight and has made it easier for them to soar through the air. It is comforting to know that if God takes care of birds in their flight, He will also take care of us as we go through life on this earth.

Dear Jesus, my Creator and Designer, help me to appreciate the wonders of birds' flight, and to learn life lessons from how You take care of birds.

THE SCIENCE OF CRIME

2 Corinthians 5:21– "God made him who had no sin to be sin for us, so that in him we might become the righteousness of God."

John 3:16– "For God so loved the world that he gave his one and only Son, that whoever believes in him shall not perish but have eternal life."

One of my favorite classes to teach was forensic science. It was a popular class, and I had to turn away some students because the class was always full. The drama and excitement of crime scene investigations fascinated many. Forensic science is the science of crime investigations. In forensic science, evidence from crime scenes is analyzed to solve a crime and to convict or absolve the suspect.

I confess that I enjoyed the labs perhaps even more than the students did. In some labs, students were divided into groups and had to create simulated crime scenes for another group to process and solve. Labs included fingerprint, hair, blood, DNA, soil, tire imprint analysis, and more. In forensic anthropology, students studied a set of bones, made several measurements, and used mathematical formulas to figure out age, race, sex, height, and cause of death. Blood spatter analysis was a bit messy, but fun in the sense that students would run around and do several physical actions to simulate various forms of blood spatter. Students used many scientific instruments, such as digital microscopes, UV light sources, precision scales, calipers, and others.

Yellow tape used in crime scene investigations

One thing I could never bring myself to do was to give students a lab on forensic entomology, which studied various steps in insect metamorphosis to figure out the approximate time of death. I took part in one such lab during a summer workshop where instructors left a 250-pound pig to rot in the summer sun so we could gather up the maggots and analyze them to decide how long the corpse had been dead. I assure you that I hardly touched my lunch that day. The year-long class was capped by a field trip the National Crime Museum in Washington DC, which has since closed and moved to another state. One exhibit was hilarious. It was about bumbling criminals and their stupid crimes and how they got caught.

The underlying goal of the class was to show that crime is a result of sin, and that sooner or later the perpetrator of the crime will be caught and prosecuted. The Bible says, " - be sure your sin will find you out" (Numbers 32:23, KJV). We all have sinned and deserve to suffer the consequences of our sins, which is death. Jesus died for all of us. He did not sin, was not guilty of any sin, but he paid the debt of our sins so that we could have eternal life.

Dear Jesus, thank You for being sin for us by dying on the cross for our sins and covering us with Your righteousness. Help us to realize how difficult that was for You and Your father, but You did it because of Your great love for us.

MAKING THINGS NEW

Revelation 21:4, 5 – "'He will wipe every tear from their eyes. There will be no more death or mourning or crying or pain, for the old order of things has passed away. He who was seated on the throne said, "I am making everything new!" Then he said, "Write this down, for these words are trustworthy and true."'

Knowledge has increased in leaps and bounds in the past 50 years. One of the technologies that has made great strides since 1981 is 3D printing. In May 1981, Dr. Hideo Kodama from Japan published details of his research, which involved printing a three-dimensional object layer by layer with a photopolymer. A photopolymer is a giant molecule that changes properties when exposed to light. Unfortunately, Kodama did not patent his discovery.

Three years later, a team of French engineers turned in a patent for stereolithography, which is a process of creating three-dimensional objects using a laser. They abandoned their patent, since they did not think it would be a successful business venture. Three weeks later, Charles Hull submitted his patent, which resulted in the release of first commercial 3D printer in 1988.

Since then, 3D printing has progressed to new and advanced devices. These devices use a nozzle to squeeze out various materials, such as plastic, metals, and even food. A special software controls the nozzle, which deposits the material layer by layer until the three-dimensional object is completed. Additive manufacturing is another name that engineers use for 3D printing. People now use 3D printing to create various objects, such toys, replacement parts for robots and other devices, car bumpers, houses, models, various plastic objects, and even food. The market for 3D printing is exploding and set to reach 50 billion dollars by 2030.

One of the most exciting things that 3D printers can do is create animal and human body parts. The use of 3D printing to fabricate body parts is bioprinting. Although most of these research projects are still in the preliminary stages, scientists and medical professionals have already printed skin, bones, muscles, blood vessels, and some small organs of the body. None have been approved for human use yet. The only human organ that has been bioprinted and transplanted is a bladder. E-nable, a small nonprofit, has been 3D printing plastic prosthetic hands for underserved populations and is now expanding to print animal prosthetics.

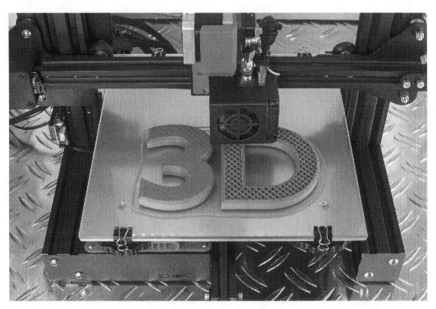

A 3D PRINTER PRINTS A LOGO ON A DIAMOND PLATE.

Although bioprinting body parts is exciting for medicine, it is used to replace body parts due to illness and disease, which are results of sin. It would be wonderful to envision a world free of sin, disease, and death. We have the assurance that this is happening soon. When Jesus comes again, he will wipe away sin from this earth, and this will include disease, pain, suffering, and death. May that day come soon!

Dear Jesus, thank You for the promise that You will make all things new. Help me to trust that You will make every part of my body new. You will give me new thoughts, new desires, new and renewed love for You, and You will banish sin forever.

HORSESHOE CRABS SAVE LIVES

1 Peter 1: 18 and 19 – "For you know that it was not with perishable things such as silver or gold that you were redeemed from the empty way of life handed down to you from your ancestors, but with the precious blood of Christ, a lamb without blemish or defect."

The fishing net was heavy–could we have caught a lot of fish? My students and I were on a scientific workboat on the Chesapeake Bay and trawling for fish for scientific studies. As the net came up with various kinds of wriggling and squirming fish, their scales glistening in the morning sun, there was this one dark creature at the bottom of the net! No wonder it was so heavy! What could it be? The students drew closer to the net, curious to see this strange creature, many of whom had never seen one before. It had a hard shell, a long spiny protuberance for a tail, and ten walking legs. There were two more small appendages close to the mouth. We had caught a horseshoe crab!

THE AUTHOR, OPHELIA BARIZO, HOLDING A
HORSESHOE CRAB ON A SCIENTIFIC SAILBOAT TRIP.
PHOTO CREDIT: OPHELIA BARIZO

Horseshoe crabs are interesting creatures. They are found in coastal areas in the Northeastern United States, with the largest populations on Delaware Bay. Something amazing happens from May to early June. The crabs swim to the beaches in hordes to lay and bury about 4,000 eggs each. Not all the eggs survive to adulthood. Shorebirds swoop down to devour the eggs. As this nature phenomenon happens, many of the horseshoe crabs are caught and brought to laboratories where scientists extract their blue blood for medical purposes.

HORSESHOE CRABS ON NEW JERSEY BEACHES ALONG
THE DELAWARE BAY DURING SPAWNING SEASON

Horseshoe blood has an enzyme called *limulus amebocyte lysate (LAL)* that thickens or coagulates when it is in the presence of bacterial toxins. Because of this unusual property, biomedical companies use the blood to test for bacterial contamination of vaccines, medicines, and medical equipment to keep these safe for people. It was used to in 2021 in the manufacture of COVID-19 vaccines, which has saved millions of lives. Horseshoe blood is so valuable that it costs $60,000 a gallon. Horseshoe blood is extracted by inserting a needle to the heart and draining about a third of its blood. The crabs are then released back to the ocean, but many crabs die, and some females do not reproduce again. ★

Just as the horseshoe crab blood has saved countless lives by finding toxins that could harm or kill us, Jesus' blood purifies us from sin. Many crabs sacrificed their lives for medicine. Jesus shed his blood and died on the cross for our eternal salvation. His blood redeems us from the taint of sin and the sting of death.

Dear Jesus, thank You for Your ultimate sacrifice for our salvation. Your blood cleanses us from our sin and guarantees us eternal life. Help us to realize how great Your sacrifice is for each one of us. I love You, Jesus, for loving me enough to shed your blood for me.

MIRACLES OF ADAPTATION

Psalm 51:10, 11 - "Create in me a pure heart, O God, and renew a steadfast spirit within me. Do not cast me from your presence or take your Holy Spirit from me."

The Garden of Eden was a paradise before sin entered into the world. The climate was perfect, just as God created it to be. There were no storms, earthquakes, or natural disasters. Animals and plants did not have diseases or pests that harmed or even killed them. Sin brought illness, death, destruction, and harsh environments to God's natural world. Living things have adaptations, processes of change that enable the organisms to be better suited or to survive in their environments. Three types of adaptations are structural, behavioral, and physiological adaptations.

A structural adaptation involves a change in body parts, texture, or color to prevent being eaten by a predator or to allow the plant to survive under harsh conditions. A snowy hare's fur is brown in the summer, but changes to white in the winter to blend with its surroundings. Succulent plants, most of which grow in the desert, have thick leaves to store water.

A behavioral adaptation is what an organism does to survive, which requires an action by the animal. Wolves hunt in packs to protect each other in an emergency, fish swim in schools since there is safety in numbers, and bears hibernate in the winter to conserve their energy.

A physiological adaptation is what happens in the internal organs or the organism's metabolism to help the organism survive in its environment. Some animals produce toxins inside their bodies to protect themselves from predators or to enable them to hunt for prey. Kangaroo rats, which live in the desert, do not drink water, but eat seeds which break down to water in their bodies. They also do not sweat and have special kidneys that allow them to survive without drinking water.

A KANGAROO RAT IN THE DESERT

The whole armor of God, which includes the helmet of salvation, the breastplate of righteousness, the shield of faith, the belt of truth, the sword of the Spirit, and feet fitted with readiness that comes from the Gospel of peace are structural adaptations to survive the onslaught of sin.

Our behavioral adaptations will help us to deal with temptations swirling around us. We need to study the Bible every day, pray to Jesus, love one another, share Jesus with our friends, and connect with God through nature.

Finally, physiological adaptations help us to survive the spiritual battle. Change needs to come from within. The right spirit begins in our hearts. Jesus is knocking at the doors of our hearts. When we let Him in, we are letting the Holy Spirit in. The Holy Spirit gives us power over sin and helps us to develop our characters to be like Christ.

Dear Father, thank You for adaptations that help living things stay alive in harsh environments. Help me to use spiritual adaptations to survive the onslaught of temptations and sin in my life. I invite the Holy Spirit to give me power over sin.

LET IT SNOW!

Isaiah 1:18 – '" Come now, let us settle the matter," says the Lord, "though your sins are like scarlet, they shall be as white as snow; though they are red as crimson, they shall be as wool."'

Who does not love a snow day? Everybody does, except if you must drive through a blinding snowstorm or get stuck in a snowdrift. Water falling from the sky is called precipitation, and it includes rain, hail, sleet, and snow. I know you agree with me that snow is the most beautiful type of precipitation because its six-sided crystals are works of art. You see these delicate, fleeting hexagons when you are driving through lightly falling snow at the right temperature. Only special techniques of photography can capture these ephemeral and beautiful works of art as permanent evidence of their breathtaking beauty.

A REAL SNOWFLAKE – PICTURE TAKEN USING
SPECIAL PHOTOGRAPHIC TECHNIQUES

The journey of a snowflake starts way above us in a cloud. A cloud is water vapor. When the temperature is right, a molecule of water sticks to an extremely tiny particle of dust or pollen and starts forming a snowflake, which is a hexagonal crystal. As the crystal falls to the ground, it changes shape all the time depending on the temperature and its path to the ground. It keeps its hexagonal structure but may acquire variations in the structure as it falls to the ground. Therefore, scientists believe that no two snowflakes are alike.

Just as no two snowflakes are alike, each one of us is unique. There is no one exactly like us in this world. Each of us can make a unique contribution to make this world a better place. Snow also reminds us that God is incredibly creative. He has made so many kinds of animals, birds, flowers, and trees in countless colors and designs. There is diversity, order, and beauty in creation.

There is a time after the beautiful colors of fall, when the trees have shed their leaves, that things look sad, dry, and drab. I always feel a sense of sadness after the leaves fall. Then comes the snow, restoring beauty to the landscape. There is a serene and happy feeling during softly falling snow. Our sinful lives are like that, but Jesus covers the ugliness of our sins with His robe of righteousness, and we become pure as snow.

Snow is important since it prepares the earth for spring. It waters the earth and makes the plants and flowers grow. The winters of our lives give us time for reflection and give us strength to face our tomorrows. So, let it snow!

My Creator and Redeemer, thank You for the snow that brightens the earth after the trees lose their beautiful foliage. The beauty of a snow crystal reminds us that we are unique and special in Your sight. Snow conveys to us how much You care for us, and how You cover our sinful hearts until we are as white as snow.

LETTING THE SUNSHINE IN

Malachi 4:2 — "But for you who revere my name, the sun of righteousness will rise with healing in its rays. And you will go out and frolic like well-fed calves."

The sun is our most important source of energy. Plants need the sun, through the process of photosynthesis, to grow and flourish. Without plants, animals will have no source of food. The sun is also responsible for warmth, weather, and wind. All other sources of energy, such as electricity, solar power, wind power, and fossil fuels depend on the sun. Without the sun, no life could exist on earth.

The sun is the center of our solar system. It is about 93,000,000 miles away from earth, and it takes eight minutes for light to travel from the sun to earth, traveling at a speed of 186,000 miles per second. The sun generates its energy through a process called nuclear fusion, where hydrogen atoms combine to produce helium atoms.

THE BRIGHT SUN ON A BLUE SKY

People from many cultures have known how important the sun is and have worshipped the sun. Some of the cultures that have worshipped the sun include the ancient Egyptians, the Incas of Peru, the Nabateans in Jordan, and the Aztecs of Mexico. They built temples to honor the sun.

After Joshua entered the Promised Land, he met several enemies. When he was fighting the battle against five different armies, he asked God to stop the sun so that the Israelites could defeat their enemies. Miraculously, God did this, and the Israelites won the battle. This story shows that nothing is too hard for the Lord. We should not hesitate to ask God to do big things. We can do great things with God's help.

Alaska has a very short growing season, but during this season the sun shines for most of the day. As a result, Alaska produces giant flowers and vegetables. A 138-pound cabbage, 65-pound cantaloupe, and 35-pound broccoli are just a few examples of the large vegetables grown in Alaska. Likewise, as we spend more time focused on the Sun of Righteousness, we will grow and flourish spiritually.

The sun also has healing powers. Sunlight improves our immune system to fight diseases, it increases mental health and makes us happy, generates vitamin D for strong bones and teeth, and kills disease-producing bacteria. We can be thankful for the sun that helps us live happy and healthful lives.

Jesus, thank You for the sun that gives us life and health. Remind us to look to the Sun (Son) of Righteousness for our spiritual and physical health.

MAGNETIC MOMENTS

John 12:3 —"And I, when I am lifted up from the earth, will draw all people to myself."

Magnets are wonderful things. Have you ever lost a ring or a coin that has fallen down a drain? A magnet can help you retrieve the lost object. Tie a small magnet to a piece of string and lower it into the drain. Pull the string slowly, and you will recover the object easily.

Magnets are metals that may attract other metals like iron, nickel, and cobalt. Combinations of metals, called alloys, can also produce magnets of varying strengths. The strongest magnets are neodymium magnets that are made of iron, boron, and a rare-earth metal called neodymium.

Magnets have two poles, north and south. Like poles repel, and unlike poles attract. The forces of a magnet do not need to touch for attraction to take place, but when you move the magnet closer, then the magnet will stick to the other metal object.

MAGNETISM AT WORK

Magnets have many uses. Parents use magnets to display their children's work on the refrigerator. A refrigerator has magnets on its doors to keep them closed. Magnets are used in compasses to find directions. Magnets are used in electronic devices, computers, microwaves, televisions, and anything that has a motor. These devices use electromagnets that wind an electric coil around a metal core.

In the field of medicine, magnets are used in MRI machines. These machines use strong magnetic fields to view internal organs and help doctors diagnose various diseases. Surgeons use magnets in surgery to remove metal shrapnel from wounds from war, accidents, and bombings. High-speed trains and roller coasters use magnetic repulsion to reduce friction with the track and propel them forward.

Animal behavior is affected by the earth's magnetic fields. Birds, butterflies, sharks, turtles, dogs, and other animals have been found to align themselves with these fields. Scientists are studying this phenomenon, but they still need to do a lot of research in this area.

When the Israelites were wandering in the desert, vipers bit them. God told Moses to build a bronze serpent and mount it on a pole. Those who looked up at the serpent were healed of their snake bites. This experience pointed to the sacrifice of Jesus on the cross. If we look up to Him, He will save us from our sins. An object acquires magnetism when it is attracted to a magnet and can draw other objects to itself and the main magnet. Jesus is the magnet that draws people to him. When we have magnetic moments with Jesus, we can also be magnets that can draw other people to him.

Lord, help me to look up to You, and be like You so that I can be a witness for You and draw people to You.

MAVEN LAUNCH

1 Corinthians 2:9 – "However, as it is written: What no eye has seen, what no ear has heard, and what no human mind has conceived - the thing God has prepared for those who love Him."

WATCHING THE COUNTDOWN TO THE MAVEN LAUNCH
PICTURE CREDIT: OPHELIA BARIZO

The year was 2013. I was serving an Albert Einstein Fellowship at the National Science Foundation near Washington, DC. The fellowship is a program where STEM teachers are chosen to serve for a year in several federal agencies at the nation's capital. It was a thrilling, wonderful year full of learning and exciting opportunities. One of the highlights was an invitation to watch the MAVEN launch at Cape Canaveral, Florida, all expenses paid. After checking into a hotel at an air force base, we visited Kennedy Space Center, viewed several wonderful exhibits, and spent some time learning about the next day's launch. MAVEN is a NASA spacecraft that was launched to orbit Mars and to collect scientific information about its atmosphere.

It was a hot and humid day on November 18, and excitement was in the air. The spacecraft was mounted on the Atlas V rocket that would propel it toward Mar's orbit. We arrived at the launch site early enough to watch the countdown that was shown on a large digital clock on a pole in front of us. We had front row seats facing the launch site, which was across the lake. As the launch grew closer, we could hear the engineers checking the systems, and then the final countdown began. As the rocket engines thrust the rocket upward, I could hear the roaring sound and felt as if the earth slightly shook on lift off. The rocket accelerated, leaving a trail of fire and smoke in the atmosphere. MAVEN was on its 10-month journey to the Red Planet! It entered Mar's orbit on September 22, 2014. MAVEN is still orbiting Mars today, sending valuable information to scientists and engineers on earth. The cost of this launch was an astronomical $582.5 million, and its extended cost would be around $20.5 million a year as it keeps orbiting Mars.

THE MAVEN SPACECRAFT ORBITING MARS
PHOTO CREDIT: NASA

I cannot imagine the amount of information MAVEN is sending to earth, not being someone who is knowledgeable about all that is going on at NASA. Mars is only a planet in our solar system, which is part of our Milky Way galaxy. It just boggles my mind to think about the tremendous amount of information in our universe, which has billions and billions of galaxies! I am just an infinitesimally tiny speck in the universe, but I know that God knows me intimately.

He is in the details of my life, and in everyone's life. He died for me that I may have salvation! That is just an awe-inspiring, awesome thought! Someday, I hope to be able travel not only to Mars, but to the farthest galaxies with God!

Dear Jesus, thank You that You are the Ruler of the Universe, and yet You know me intimately, all the details of my life, and You love me for who I am. Thank You for Your promise of the place that You have prepared for those who love You.

MIND-CONTROLLED PROSTHETICS

Romans 12:2 – "Do not conform to the pattern of this world, but be transformed by the renewing of your mind. Then you will be able to test and approve what God's will is – his good, pleasing, and perfect will."

Our hands and feet are wonderful instruments that enable us to explore nature, perform chores around the house, and just enjoy life. Unfortunately, some people lose their limbs in war, vehicle accidents, natural disasters, explosions, and even from disease. This loss can be very devastating since it can limit mobility and functionality. What would we do without our limbs?

Mind-controlled prosthetic limbs allow patients to use their arms through nerve impulses transmitted from their brains to their remaining muscles. These modern prosthetic limbs can even feel textures and grip objects. Pretty amazing! There is a downside – the cost, since these devices may cost up to hundreds of thousands of dollars.

Using a prosthetic hand to work on the computer

When the pandemic struck in 2020, seventeen-year-old Benjamin Choi, who was in the tenth grade in Virginia, decided to put his spare time to good use. He took the time to build a mind-controlled robotic arm! He had seen a documentary on these special prosthetics when he was ten years old, but he wanted to build one that did not require expensive and painful surgery to implant sensors on the brain and change the muscles to receive the commands.

Benjamin worked up to 16 hours a day on a Ping-Pong table in his basement where he designed the arm and used an inexpensive 3D printer to print several pieces of the arm. He then connected the pieces with fishing line. It took 75 iterations for Benjamin to produce his $300 device. With his coding experience he developed an algorithm for the arm to be driven by artificial intelligence (AI). Benjamin's invention has won him many awards. He has also won funding to further his research and perfect his arm with several engineers. He believes his invention could also be used to control other devices, such as wheelchairs, and help patients with Lou Gehrig's disease to communicate.

Our brains control so many of our body functions, including mobility. There needs to be important and constant connections between mind and body for best health and enjoyment. Just as the brain needs the axons and dendrites to communicate with the rest of the body, we need to have constant connection to God to grow spiritually and to carry out His will in our lives. An active, growing Christian calls for having a vibrant connection to the mind of God, just like the branches are connected to the Vine. Jesus said in John 15:5 – "I am the vine; you are the branches. If you remain in me and I in you, you will bear much fruit; apart from me you can do nothing."

Dear God, thank You for my marvelous brain that controls my actions, my words, and my thoughts. Thank You that my brain also receives the wonderful sensations and information from the beautiful world you created for me. Help me to have a constant connection with You, so that I may grow to be more like You.

MUSHROOM ENGINEERING

Acts 1:8 - "But you will receive power when the Holy Spirit comes on you; and you will be my witnesses in Jerusalem, and in all Judea and Samaria, and to the ends of the earth."

People have been fascinated by mushrooms throughout history. At times, there was a mysterious element to this fascination. Mushrooms have also been despised, kicked around the trails in the forest, and regarded by some people with trepidation. During the pandemic, increased interest in foraging has also resulted in increased interest in mushrooms, especially the wild edible ones. As people learned more about mushrooms, some of their mysteries have decreased.

Scientists and engineers are finding enormous amounts of information about mushrooms and are exploring innovative ways to use mushrooms, such as mushroom foam, mushroom packaging, and even sustainable buildings. Much of these are still the subjects of further research and experimentation, but the lowly mushroom is fast establishing itself as a new source of materials.

The incredible power of mushrooms was harnessed by two young students at Rennselaer Polytechnic Institute, Kevin McIntyre and Eben Mayer, as a class project. They grew fungus under their beds to make mushroom foam as an alternative to Styrofoam. They used mycelia, the rapidly growing root-like structures of fungi, and a binding agent to make their inventions. They started a company called Ecovative to mass-produce their creations. Their initial products were packing materials for computers and glass bottles. They have since branched out to other products such as furniture cushions, stools, mushroom leather, mushroom meat substitutes, mushroom fashions, and do-it-yourself products. The neat thing about these products is that you can just put them in the garden if you don't need them anymore, and they biodegrade into the soil. This makes it have a lower environmental footprint than various kinds of plastics.

Other researchers and companies have subsequently taken on the challenge of developing more unique and sustainable mushroom merchandise. Philip Ross, an artist in the Bay Area, started working with mushroom mycelia to produce mushroom leather, which he called Reishi after a type of mushroom. He enlisted the help of Sophia Wang, a doctoral student, and they both started a biotech company called Mycoworks, which now produces sheets of Reishi for leather products. The company now has 75 patents and over 160 employees in three countries. High-end companies, such as Hermes and GM Ventures have collaborated with Mycoworks for their products. The lowly mushroom is fast becoming an inspiration for a variety of commercial products that benefit humanity.

A VEGAN LEATHER WALLET MADE
FROM MUSHROOM MYCELIUM

Jesus chose several poor, lowly, and uneducated men to be his apostles. When these men were imbued with the Holy Spirit, they accomplished so much for the spread of the gospel during their time. Like them, we can receive power to be useful wherever we are. God can use each of us mightily to make a difference in the lives of many.

Dear Jesus, just like the lowly mushroom can be useful in so many ways, help me to use my many talents to be a witness for You. Please infuse me with the Holy Spirit so that I can make a difference even in only one life and bring that person to know and love You.

ALL EYES ON YOU

Psalm 119:18 - "Open my eyes that I may behold wonderful things from your law."

Did you know that your eyes are so important that seeing requires more than fifty percent of your brain's function? That means more than half of your brain is used to process information received through your eyes! Eyes are so remarkable that they have seven million cones to detect different colors and one hundred million rods for vision in the dark. They also have over two million parts that help you see. The eye muscles are also extremely fast. The phrase "in the blink of an eye" makes more sense since the eye can blink fifteen to twenty times a minute.

Animals have incredible eyes, too! A dragonfly has 360-degree vision, but more astonishing is that each eye has 100 million ommatidia, tiny lenses with mirror-like surfaces that are so sensitive to movements. Have you tiptoed behind a dragonfly to catch it only to have it fly away just as you were trying to pinch your fingers to catch its tail? It's because dragonflies have eyes behind their heads!

DRAGONFLY EYE HAS MANY SMALLER LENSES

Some animals have adorable, large eyes which are unique and interesting. A tree frog has large, bulging eyes that also act as its defense. It's called "startle coloration." When frog closes its eyes, it blends with its leafy environment. If a predator comes close, it suddenly opens its eyes, startling the predator momentarily, which allows the frog to escape. A chameleon has large, colorful eyes that can fully rotate and even allow it to focus on two different things at the same time. Tarsiers, rare mammals found in the Philippine rain forests, have the largest eyes compared to their body size. Each eye is almost as large as its brain. Owls, which are nocturnal animals, have special eyes that can see in the dark. Since the owls can't move their eyes, they must rotate their necks to see their prey better.

God, who created the wonders of this world, created our eyes to see and appreciate nature. What would we do without our eyes? Our eyes can see varied colors, beautiful landscapes, the faces of those we love, and the marvels of nature. We can read His Word and learn more about God with our eyes.

Proverbs 15:3 says, "The eyes of the Lord are everywhere, keeping watch on the evil and the good." His eyes are also on the righteous and attentive to all our needs. (Psalm 34:15). We can be thankful that the eyes of the Lord are in every place. God is all-seeing. He watches the evil and the good. He sees evil and protects us from it. It is wonderful to know that God sees me – He knows the number of hairs on my head, and your head. He can see into our hearts. He sees the past and sees into the future–and He knows what is best for us. Aren't you happy that God sees us–and no matter what He sees about us, He loves us just the same?

Dear God, thank You for the gift of vision. Help me to see the good in this world and others. Thank You also that Your eyes are always on us, and You see everything about us — the good and the bad, yet You love us with an unconditional love.

ORIGAMI MAGIC

Isaiah 64:8 – "Yet, O Lord, you are our father. We are the clay, you are the potter, we are all the work of your hand."

Visions of leaves sprouting from seeds and the opening and closing of flowers using time-lapse photography are fascinating. Origami, the traditional Japanese art of paper folding, has derived a lot of inspiration from nature and is now being used in engineering applications. The folding and unfolding of structures in nature is inspiring engineers, mathematicians, and architects to develop structures that are self-assembling and foldable.

Scientists and engineers are creating structures that fold and unfold, bend, and twist or change shape in response to pressure, heat, or electricity. Origami is now used in robotics, pharmacology, the military, the airline industry, the space industry, and in medicine. Engineers have teamed up with origami artists to create dwellings that can fold when not in use and unfold when ready for use. The homeless and refugees can use these dwellings since they are light and portable. Robots can change shape and adapt to tight spaces in collapsed buildings during rescue operations. Rockets can take folded solar arrays in their payload bays, which can be unfurled in space to supply solar energy for flight. Biomedical engineers turn to origami to design heart stents and catheters for use in medicine. Teachers use origami in schools. The act of folding builds concentration, manual dexterity, and creativity. The many potential uses of origami have spawned research and funding in this interesting field.

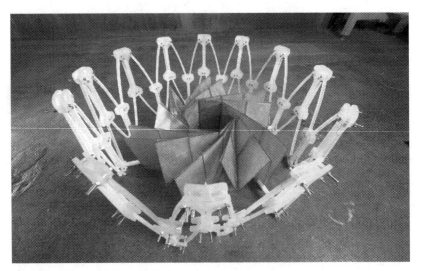

AN ORIGAMI SOLAR ARRAY
PICTURE CREDIT: NSF MEDIA

Nature has supplied scientists, engineers, mathematicians, and architects the perfect models for designing origami products. They must examine intimately the designs in nature to be able to mimic them. The science of biomimetics imitates nature to develop materials and processes that solve human problems.

The Master Designer created flowers, trees, and animals for us to enjoy, inspire engineers to deal with problems, and help us and live life to the fullest. As the field of origami engineering has endless amazing possibilities, so does our life when we entrust it to God. He can do more for us when we are willing to be molded by Him. In a modern sense, we can be origami in the hands of God, folded, unfolded, and shaped according to His purpose for our lives.

Dear Father, thank You for Your created works that give us joy and help solve our problems. Help me to trust You to be molded, folded, and shaped according to Your will, so that we may fulfill Your purpose for us in this world.

PLUG INTO THE POWER!

Ephesians 3:20 – "Now to Him who is able to do immeasurably more than all we ask or imagine according to his power that is at work within us."

Electricity is ubiquitous and indispensable! Electricity powers our lights, home appliances, industries, entertainment, medical equipment, computers, and a host of other things. What would we do without electricity? When the power is out, we feel it acutely and desperately.

There are several sources of electricity. Most of our electricity comes from the burning of fossil fuels, most notably coal. The heat energy produced boils water which runs turbines that convert mechanical energy to electrical energy. Solar power from the sun is collected in panels hooked up to photovoltaic cells that convert solar energy to electricity. The wind turns windmills attached to generators that transform wind energy into electricity. Waterfalls harness the mechanical energy of flowing water to run turbines to generate electricity. Radioactive materials release large amounts of energy through nuclear fission which heats up steam to run turbines that produce electrical energy.

HIGH–VOLTAGE ELECTRICAL TOWERS

Electricity is the flow of electrons. Circuits transfer electrons from the power source to your electrical appliances and back to the source. For the transfer to be complete the circuit needs to be closed, which means there is a continuous path, or loop, of wires from the power source and back. If the circuit is interrupted by a switch, power will not flow. Interrupting the flow of electrons is also done by unplugging the appliance or turning it off. Plugging it back in completes the circuit and restores the power.

When the Israelites found themselves between the advancing Egyptian army and the Red Sea, they were frightened for their lives. God showed His power through Moses. He asked Moses to stretch his hand over the sea. The sea parted, allowing the Israelites to pass through on dry land. When they were on the other side, and the Egyptian army was advancing quickly on the dry land, Moses stretched forth his hand again, and the enemy was covered and washed into the sea.

There were so many instances when God showed His power to His people in Bible times. He is still showing His power even now, the power of healing, the power to calm storms in our lives, the power to change lives, and the power to answer our prayers. We need to plug into that power and stay connected to Him to do His will in our lives. With His power in our lives, we can do great things and overcome sin.

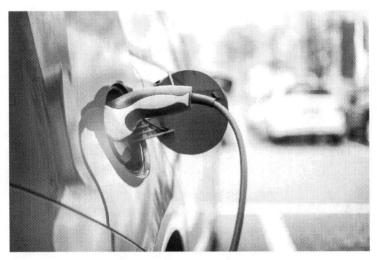

AN ELECTRIC CAR PLUGS INTO THE POWER.

Dear Jesus, help me to stay connected to You so that I can harness Your power in my life to overcome sin, solve my problems, and be what You want me to be.

ROBOTIC REALITIES

Psalm 139:14 — "I will praise you because I am fearfully and wonderfully made; your works are wonderful; I know that full well."

Psalm 143: 10 — "Teach me to do Your will, For You are my God; May your good Spirit lead me on level ground."

Robots do lots of things. They help build cars, vacuum your home, do jobs that require repeated movements, go into a collapsed building to find survivors, perform surgery, explore the surface of Mars, and do things that may be unsafe or boring for humans to do. Robots are very important, have become indispensable, and some may even save lives.

Robots may appear to be very smart because of all the things that they can do. In reality they can't do what they do without a human telling them what to do. Robots' brains need to be programmed to do their jobs by humans. There are people who write computer code to get robots to perform certain functions. During robotic surgery, surgeons use a computer to get the robot to perform surgery. With sophisticated robots, they can get to parts of the body that are difficult to get to. They can even insert cameras to see body parts or tumors in greater detail.

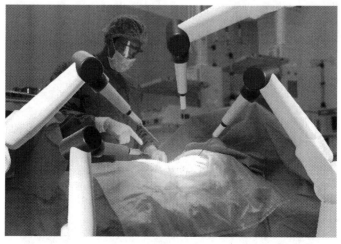

A ROBOTIC SURGERY MACHINE ALLOWS DOCTORS
TO PERFORM COMPLEX PROCEDURES

Unlike robots, who need to be programmed by humans, we have been created with a mind within a brain, which is capable of higher order thinking skills. Our minds can think and make intelligent decisions. God made us to be creative, imaginative, innovative, and problem solvers. We are made to have thoughts and feelings, which robots don't have. Thank God for our wonderful brains, and that we are marvelously made.

Have you ever been spied on by a robot? Singapore has used trial robots to patrol the streets, watch people's behavior and warn them of "undesirable social behavior." The robots are supposed to help police keep track of minor violations. These robots are equipped with seven cameras and microphones. They speak warnings to people who may park bicycles in the wrong way, are not social distancing, or who are smoking.

We do not need robots to patrol our behavior. God has given us a conscience to help us to know right from wrong. Besides, God sees everything we do. Nothing is hidden from Him. He even sees into our hearts and knows our thoughts. We do not need a robot to warn us in a funny voice that we are doing unacceptable behavior. God has given us the Holy Spirit to impress us to do the right things.

Dear God, help me do what is right in Your sight and thank You for the Holy Spirit who guides me every day.

SEEING GOD THROUGH OUR SENSES

Philippians 4:8 – "Finally, brothers and sisters, whatever is true, whatever is noble, whatever is right, whatever is pure, whatever is lovely, whatever is admirable—if anything is excellent or praiseworthy—think about such things."

One spring night a bear yanked our trash can out of its bearings and scattered trash all over our backyard. A couple of nights later, it happened again! Our trash bin was toppled over with all its trash and trash was scattered all over the lawn. To make matters worse, the bear pulled down bird feeders that were hanging from a strong wire between two trees. "This can't happen again," my husband muttered. He bought a solar-powered motion sensor that barks like a dog when there is an intruder nearby. We have not had bear incidents since then, but we may have to get another sensor for the front yard for deer that nibble on our Hosta plants.

A TRASH-LOVING BEAR

A sensor is a device that monitors its environment and turns what it senses into electrical signals that may be measured, felt, or heard. An actuator turns these electrical signals into physical outputs. When the motion sensor detects motion from the bear, it sends the signal to the actuator which physically barks like a dog to scare the bear away.

We use several different kinds of sensors these days—sensors that detect motion, temperature, pressure, light, smoke, carbon dioxide, gas, pollution, and other things. Sensors help protect us from poisonous substances, help us control our heating systems to make us more comfortable, and drive away animal intruders!

Did you know that our bodies are equipped with sensors? We have five different senses—sight, hearing, taste, smell, and touch. Our senses gather information from our environment and send these to our brains. Our brains process the information and react to the various stimuli from our environment. In most cases the reaction is instantaneous due to electrical currents carrying the impulses from our brains. God wonderfully creates us to be sensors and actuators.

Our senses are avenues to our brain, our minds, and souls. Since the information we get from our senses determines how we react, respond, and live our lives, it is so important to select which type of information we feed our minds with. I will paraphrase what the Chinese philosopher Lao Tzu once said—our thoughts become words, words become actions, actions become habits, habits become character, and character decides destiny. How we receive, interpret, and react to information from our environment eventually decides our destiny.

Dear Lord, help me to choose what I put into my senses, and only choose what is pure, holy, lovely, and admirable.

SMART CONTACT LENSES

1 Corinthians 10:31– "So whether you eat or drink or whatever you do, do it all for the glory of God."

3 John 1:2– "Dear friend, I pray that you may enjoy good health and that all may go well with you, even as your soul is getting along well."

Did you know that smart contact lenses can measure sugar levels in eyes? The lenses are being developed and tested on rabbits and one human by researchers at Stanford University and Pohang University of Science and Technology in South Korea. Why is that so important? The lenses measure the amount of glucose in tears and send the data wirelessly to a cell phone, where it can be viewed using an app. No more painful finger sticks to track blood sugar! If successful, it will be a less invasive way to track blood sugar levels.

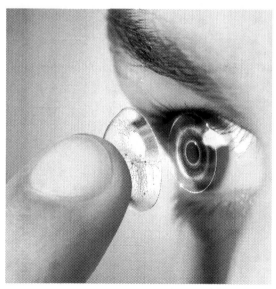

SMART CONTACT LENSES CAN TRACK SUGAR LEVELS.

Diabetes is one of the most prevalent diseases in the USA. Recent 2023 statistics show that 37.3 million Americans have diabetes, and 96 million have prediabetes. Diabetes is a disease that affects how the body uses glucose. Glucose is a simple sugar that supplies energy for the body and fuel for brain cells. The source of this sugar is carbohydrates, which break down to glucose during the digestive process. Glucose ends up in the blood, where it provides energy to the tissues of the body. Diabetes results when there is too much sugar in the blood. Under normal conditions, the hormone insulin gets the glucose out of the blood to the cells, where it provides energy. In diabetes, the body does not make enough insulin, so the sugar builds up in the blood and it is not used efficiently by the cells.

Chronic high blood sugar can cause serious health problems, such as blurry vision, blindness, nerve damage, kidney disease, infections due to decreased immune functions, and cardiovascular problems. When a person can effectively check blood sugar it makes it easier to make life changes to reverse the effect of diabetes in the body. Life changes include eating a healthy diet, regular physical activity, and exploring ways to manage stress effectively. These habits lead to health and wellness of body and mind which will glorify God, our Maker.

Dear Jesus, thank You for fruits, vegetables, nuts, and seeds that You provide for our food. Help us to eat well, exercise each day, and trust in You so that we may achieve and maintain good health for Your glory.

THESE SHOES HELP THE BLIND "SEE"

Psalm 146:8 – "The Lord gives sight to the blind, the Lord lifts up those who are bowed down, the Lord loves the righteous."

There is great news for the blind. Scientists have created smart shoes that help the blind "see," or make it easier for people who are visually impaired. The shoes have waterproof sensors attached to each tip that send signals warning the wearer of rocks, snow poles, or other obstacles on the path. They also help the wearer turn left or right.

The shoes, with the trade name InnoMake, can detect particles up to ten feet away and send vibrations directly to shoes or make noises to warn visually impaired or blind persons. The shoe sensors send messages directly to a person's smartphone or through special headphones. Sensors can also transmit messages through bright LED lights to warn of obstacles or dangers in the dark. It also prevents being rammed or jolted by the wearer's cane when running into an obstacle.

SPECIAL SHOES THAT HELP THE BLIND "SEE"
PICTURE CREDIT: INNOVATE

The Bible tells us several stories of Jesus healing the blind. A man blind from birth could see again after Jesus put spit on the man's eye. Jesus also healed Bartimaeus, a blind beggar who was sitting by the roadside and called out to Him. Jesus said to him, "Go your way, your faith had made you whole." When we get to heaven, the blind will be able to see clearly. The use of these sensors will not be necessary. Not only will the blind see, but the lame will walk again. All our diseases and illnesses will be wiped away. It will be a wonderful and glorious day for people who have been ravaged by illness and handicapped from various physical impairments!

Jesus can also heal our spiritual blindness. A lot of our sins are a result of spiritual blindness. Just as Jesus made the blind man see, He can also help us see the results of our sins. We will appreciate more fully the salvation that He gives us through His ultimate sacrifice on the cross. He died so that we may be healed and released from the guilt of sin! He died to make us free from the results of sin! His sacrifice will heal us physically, emotionally, and spiritually!

Dear Jesus, please heal my spiritual blindness so I can see Your love and care for me. Help me to see the many blessings You have given me and the promise of eternal life through You.

THE JAMES WEBB TELESCOPE

Psalm 8:3,4– "When I consider your heavens, the work of your fingers, the moon and the stars, which you have set in place, what is mankind that you are mindful of them, human beings that you care for them?"

Stars twinkled in the dark sky as we settled on our mats on the grass. I was part of a church group of youngsters belonging to a Pathfinder Club. We earned honors in this club, and I was working toward an astronomy badge. This was one of the several nights that we would gaze up at the sky, learn about the constellations and their places in the night sky. We did not have a telescope to scan the night sky then, but today we have all kinds of telescopes to give us a better picture of the heavens.

The James Webb Space Telescope (JWST) is a joint project by NASA, the European Space Agency, and the Canadian Space Agency, and has involved more than 300 universities and organizations in 29 states and 14 countries. It was launched on December 25, 2021, and is the most powerful telescope ever. It is more powerful than the Hubble Telescope, launched in 1990, and which is still orbiting the earth. The JWST is so much further out in space than the Hubble. The $10 billion telescope is nearly a million miles away from earth. It traveled to space on a rocket. Unlike the Hubble Telescope that is orbiting the earth, the JWST is orbiting the sun at a space called Langrange point 2 (L2). The telescope has already been sending astounding pictures of the universe, including the Carina Nebula, faraway galaxies, and hundreds of stars that scientists have never seen before. It is still sending stunning pictures of the universe that are very exciting to see. Some of the pictures and data the telescope is sending to earth are challenging well-established theories of the universe. There is still an incredible amount of information that researchers and scientists do not know or understand about the universe.

THE JAMES WEBB TELESCOPE EXPLORES
FARAWAY GALAXIES.

Deep space is still puzzling to many, but this we know: that the Creator knows all about of what is going on in vast expanse of space. The Bible says in Psalm 19:1 – "The heavens declare the glory of God; the skies proclaim the work of his hands." When we look up to the heavens, we marvel at God's tremendous and awe-inspiring creative power. He controls the motions of the galaxies and the countless stars. The revolutions and rotations of the heavenly bodies are in perfect order and mathematical precision. We have nothing to fear or be concerned about anything in our lives since we know that God is in control of everything.

Our Creator and King, thank You for the vast Universe that You have created. Thank You for the moon and stars that brighten the night sky for me. Thank You for the reminder that You care for me, and I need not worry, for You are in control of the universe and everything in my life.

THE LOST IS FOUND

Luke 15:7– "I tell you that in the same way there will be more rejoicing in heaven over one sinner who repents than over ninety-nine righteous persons who do not need to repent."

Microchips are everywhere. Microchips are "the building blocks of technology." They are in all our electronic devices, from household appliances, cars, medical scanners, fitness trackers, computers, and smartphones. People can also have microchips surgically implanted between the thumb and index finger. A microchip has miniscule electrical circuits etched on a small wafer of silicon, which is made from sand. It is mind-boggling that a microchip the size of your fingernail contains billions of tiny transistors that function as switches to turn current on and off.

Have you ever lost a pet? Pets are getting lost every day, but now there is hope for lost pets. A hypodermic needle implants a chip under the dog's skin between shoulder bones. A pet can now have inserted into its skin a microchip the size of a grain of rice, which contains its owner's contact information. Animal shelters and veterinarians have scanners that extract information from pet microchips. Lost pets taken to these places have a more likely chance of being found since their owners can be contacted from the information in their microchips.

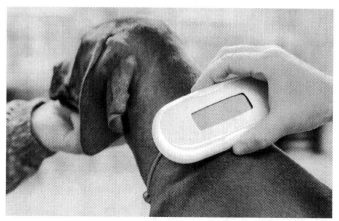

A VET CHECKS A MICROCHIP IMPLANT UNDER A PUPPY.

Jesus told the parable of the lost sheep to a group tax collectors, sinners, Pharisees, and teachers of the law. He told them of a shepherd who had a hundred sheep but had lost one of them. The shepherd searched high and low for the lost sheep and was so happy when he found it. He said that in the same way, the Father will search for the lost until they are found, for He is not willing that any should perish.

We are never lost to God. He always knows where we are. We may feel we are lost sometimes, but God will always find us. His eyes are always on us. We do not need microchips imbedded in our hands for God to find us. He is all-seeing, all-knowing, and can even read our innermost thoughts and feelings. He will go to the ends of the earth to find us and save us if we allow Him to. And when a sinner is found, He rejoices like a shepherd who finds the one lost sheep.

Dear Jesus, thank You that I am never lost to You. Help me also to seek You and find You and allow You to come into my heart and dwell in me.

THE WONDROUS PROTON

3 John 1:2 - "Dear friend, I pray that you may enjoy good health and that all may go well with you, even as your soul is getting along well."

One day in April 2020, I got a phone call from my doctor that jolted me to my core and changed my life. "Your tumor is malignant. You have soft-tissue sarcoma," he said haltingly and kindly, to soften the impact, I suppose. A small lump on the left side of my knee, which I had for more than two years, and was considered harmless by other doctors, turned out to be sarcoma.

After a series of scans, medical tests, and a difficult biopsy, I had to undergo two painful surgeries, and six weeks later, a series of 30 proton therapy treatments. Every day we had to drive to Baltimore to receive treatment. The technologists made a mold for my leg to prevent motion during the treatment, which surprisingly and fortunately was painless. Due to a combination of both treatments, and what I believe was an answer to the prayers of many and God's healing, I am now free from the disease.

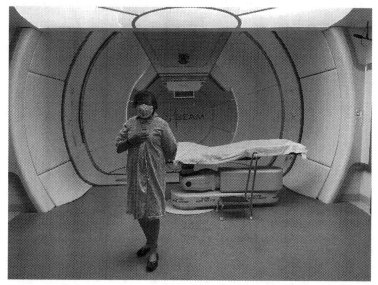

THE AUTHOR POSES BEFORE PROTON THERAPY TREATMENT.
PHOTO CREDIT: ELIZABETH HOWE

Atoms are made of protons, electrons, and neutrons. Protons are the positively charged particles in an atom. In proton therapy, protons are used to destroy cancer cells. Hydrogen gas is injected into a metal cylinder, which is surrounded by an electrical field that extracts the protons. These protons are speeded up by a cyclotron to incredible speeds almost the speed of light. Electromagnets then focus the beam to the treatment room where the radiation is directed at the tumor site to kill the cells. Because the beam points directly at the tumor, damage to surrounding cells is spared, and the side effects of radiation are minimal. The beam damages the tumor's DNA so that the tumor is not able to repair itself or grow new cells.

The atom can unleash a lot of energy and power and may be harnessed for the benefit of mankind. The power of proton therapy has helped thousands of people with life-threatening cancer. It has prolonged lives, cured many people, and improved the quality of life for a lot of cancer patients. Likewise, the power of healing of the Great Physician has given hope and life to many. We can trust in God's healing power not only to heal bodies but also to heal minds.

Dear Jesus, help me to trust in You when I am overwhelmed with the pain of body or mind. I know that You have the power to banish aches and pains of body and spirit. Thank You for the promise that You will take care of us, sustain us, and restore our bodies and souls.

THE SCIENCE OF SCENT

1Thessalonians 5:16-18 (NIV) – *"Rejoice always, pray continually, give thanks in all circumstances; for this is God's will for you in Christ Jesus."*

Smell is one of our most memorable senses. The sense of smell goes along with your sense of taste. When the food smells good, it almost always tastes good, too. When the food smells bad, it makes you lose your appetite. The bad smell also warns you that the food may not be good to eat anymore and may even make you sick if you eat it. Humans can identify at least one trillion different smells because of the approximately 10 million smell receptors in everyone's nose. It is said that humans can also smell fear, happiness, and even sexual arousal.

Dogs have a much more developed smell than humans. Research has shown that dogs can even sniff out feelings and can tell when a child is stressed or is about to have a meltdown. Dogs can detect various forms of cancer, narcolepsy, epileptic seizures, blood sugar, and other forms of illnesses.

COVID-19 detection with dogs

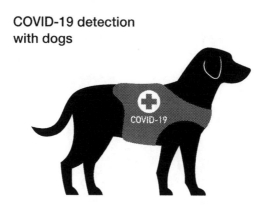

DOGS CAN DETECT CORONAVIRUS.

During the pandemic, dogs have been used to detect COVID-19. There is a training facility in Greencastle, Pennsylvania, that trains the dogs to identify people with COVID-19. After training for five days, they can detect the disease with up to 95% accuracy. Dogs may detect COVID from a person's mask, but also from sweat. Using dogs is less invasive than sticking a Q-tip up your nose. Scientists are now training dogs to detect long COVID.

God has given us the sense of smell to enjoy the various things He has made for us—sweet-smelling flowers, fruits, and all the wonderful aromas from the food we eat. He has also given us our sense of smell to warn us of things that are dangerous to us.

On another note, there are aromas from us that are very pleasing to the Lord. Revelation 5:8 says – "each one had a harp and they were holding bowls full of incense, which are the prayers of the God's people." God loves the aroma of our prayers. He always listens and answers when we talk to Him.

Thank you, God, for giving us our sense of smell that makes us enjoy life better. Help us to send You the aromas of our prayers. We know that You love to listen and answer our prayers according to Your will.

WINDY WONDERS

Isaiah 43:2 – "When you pass through the waters, I will be with you; and when you pass through the rivers, they will not sweep over you. When you walk through the fire, you will not be burned; the flames will not set you ablaze."

Wind is moving air. Wind may come to us as a delightful breeze, a strong gust, a windstorm, a tornado, or a hurricane. It can be refreshing, but it can also be frightening. Air is composed of 21% oxygen, 78% nitrogen, and 1% of other gases. We need oxygen in the air for life. Nitrogen, which is inert, prevents oxygen from burning and supplies nutrients to humans in the form of proteins.

The sun plays an important part of wind. The sun heats up various surfaces in the earth differently. These differences in heat cause variations in pressure. When air in high pressure areas moves to lower pressure, wind is formed. Sometimes, when the differences are great, storms can be the result of these movements, especially if accompanied by rain or snow.

Wind is important since it can supply energy for our industries and homes. It is also important for a lot of wind sports that we enjoy. Many sports activities such as sailing, hang gliding, kiteboarding, windsurfing, and others make use of the wind.

Although we can get a lot of benefits from the wind, sometimes wind causes a lot of devastation, such as injury, death, and destruction of property. People cannot calm these ravaging windstorms, but Jesus can. The disciples and Jesus were in a boat when a strong storm came upon them. The disciples were afraid, but Jesus said, "Why are ye fearful, O ye of little faith? Then he arose and rebuked the winds and the sea, and there was a great calm." (Matthew 8:26, KJV).

PALM TREES WAVING IN A WINDY TROPICAL STORM.

Sometimes in our lives we feel the storms of temptation, disease, family problems, and other problems. Sometimes these storms get so strong that we feel we cannot survive them, but Jesus can calm the storms in our lives as He calmed the storms in the sea. He is stronger than the wind and the storms in our lives. We can trust Him to get us over these storms.

Dear Jesus, please help me fight the winds of temptations and other storms in my life. Help me calm the storms and keep me in Your love.

YOU MAY EAT YOUR FOOD WRAPPER!

Genesis 1:29 – "'Then God said, "I give you every seed-bearing plant on the face of the whole earth and every tree that has fruit with seed in it. They will be yours for food."'

Every day, tons of plastic pollution go into landfills, oceans, and even forests. People use two million plastic bags every minute in the world. That is an enormous amount of plastic. Seventy-five percent of beach litter is plastic. It includes a lot of water bottles. Did you know that one million plastic bottles are bought every minute and will continue to increase in the future? Plastic harms marine life— fish, turtles, sharks, dolphins, and coral reefs. Plastic also harms us. Extremely tiny plastic particles called microplastics can enter the body and cause a lot of problems, such as inflammation, high blood pressure, and even cancers.

Food manufacturers use an inordinate number of plastics in food wraps. To reduce the amount of plastic packaging some food companies have come up with edible plastic wrappers. There is an ice cream sandwich that has an edible wrap made of potato starch. A company in Brazil makes edible hamburger wraps, so you can just get your burger from the takeout and bite into the burger, wrap and all. An edible wrap is made from various materials such as mushrooms, algae, seaweed, potato starch, and rice paper. Much of it is tasteless or assumes the taste of the food item it comes in.

DELICIOUS SPRING ROLLS WRAPPED IN RICE PAPER

Much of the food that is wrapped in plastic or edible wraps is manufactured food. Sadly, manufactured food is loaded with sugar, artificial ingredients, and chemicals that could cause health problems, such as diabetes, high blood pressure, and cancer. God has provided us with natural foods that are better for our health. He has given us grains, fruits, nuts, and vegetables. Daniel and his three friends did not partake of the food of the King, but instead asked only for vegetables and water for ten days. At the end of ten days, they were found to be healthier than all who ate the king's food. We would be healthier if we stick as much as possible to God's diet.

Thank You, God, for all the wonderful food You have given us for our health. Help us choose wisely and have more fruits and vegetables in our diet to be healthier and happier.

ABOUT THE AUTHOR

Ophelia Barizo is an experienced, award winning, successful educator with four decades of innovative STEM classroom teaching. She is a Nationally Certified STEM Educator through the National Institute of STEM Education (NISE) and has served as an Albert Einstein Distinguished Educator Fellow, Engineering Directorate (ENG), at the National Science Foundation (NSF). She has also won several National Science Teachers Association (NSTA) awards including the Toyota Tapestry Award for Teachers, Making a Difference Award, and STEM Educator of the Year Award. She was a Columbia Union Educator of the Year and was also awarded the Environmental Educator Award from the Chesapeake Bay Trust. In 2021 Ophelia was awarded the STEM Educator of the Year Award by Loma Linda University EXSEED. Ophelia is experienced in STEM professional development, curriculum development, program development, grant-writing, and organization of STEM outreach activities. Ophelia's passion is discipling students to Christ through STEM and pointing students to the Creator of the Universe.

END NOTES

"Burdoch Thistle." Kids Answers in Genesis. May 15, 2018. https://answersingenesis.org/kids/science/biomimicry/burdock-thistle/

"Experimental Newborn Bandages Inspired by Spider Webs, Mica and Gecko Feet." *Huff Post.* November 2, 2012. https://www.huffpost.com/entry/newborn-bandages-spider-webs-mica_n_2058677.

"Trading Dress-Up for Lift-Off, Barbie Flies on Space Station for First Time." Collect Space. April 14, 2022. http://www.collectspace.co,/news/news-041422-barbie-dolls-space-station-mission-dreamstar.html.

"Honeycomb: One of Nature's Most Beautiful and Useful Structures," Best Bees. November 21, 2022. https://bestbees.com/2022/11/21/honeycomb/.

Georgiou, Aristos. "How Burmese Pythons Invaded Florida with 100,000 Now Roaming the Everglades." Newsweek. June 29, 2022. https://www.newsweek.com/burmese-pythons-invaded-florida-100000-roaming-everglades-1720356.

"Kudzu: The Invasive Vine that Ate the South." The Nature Conservancy. August 9, 2019. https://www.nature.org./en-us/about-us/

where-we-work/united-states/indiana/stories-in-indiana/ludzu-invasive-species.

*Indonesian Village Turns Unwanted Trash into Robot COVID Helper. "New York Post. August 11, 2021. https://nypost.com/2021/08/11/indonesian-village-turns-unwanted-trash-into-robot-covid-helper/.

Charleston, Haley. "Plummer, Permobil's Explorer Mini Recognized In TIME Magazine's Top 100 Best Inventions of 2021." Belmont Univeristy. April 8, 2022. https://news.belmont.edu/plummer-permobils-explorer-mini-recognized-in-time-magazines-top-100-best-inventions-of-2021/

Mathiesen, Karl. "The Junk Orchestra: Making Music Out of a Landfill." *The Guardian.* July 13, 2015. https://www.theguardian.com/global-development-professionals-network/2015/jul/13/junk-recycled-orchestra-paraguay-music-landfill

"Kids in Paraguay Make Music Out of Trash." *Washington Post.* February 19, 2013. https://www.washingtonpost.com/lifestyle/kidspost/kids-in-paraguay-make-music-out-of-trash/2013/02/15/c57390b2-486b-11e2-b6f0-e851e741d196_story.html

Tsioulcas, Anastasia. "From Trash to Triumph: The Recycled Orchestra." MPR News. September 15, 2016. https://www.mprnews.org/story/2016/09/15/npr-from-trash-to-triumph-the-recycled-orchestra

"Mr. Trash Wheel: A Proven Solution to Ocean Plastics." Mr. Trash Wheel. Accessed June 4, 2023. https://www.mrtrashwheel.com/.

"How Does GPS Work?" NASA Science Space Place. June 27, 2019. https://spaceplace.nasa.gov/gps/en/

Prisco, Jacopo. "Why Modern Airplanes Have Winglets." CNN. April 13, 2022. https://www.cnn.com/travel/article/airplane-winglets-cmd/index.html

3dsourced. "The Complete History of 3D Printing: From 1980 to 2023. https://www.3dsourced.com/guides/history-of-3d-printing.

"The Many Ways Horseshoe Crab Blood Will Amaze You." American Oceans. Accessed June 4, 2023. https://www.americanoceans.org/blog/horseshoe-crab-blood/

"Sun Facts." The Planets. Accessed June 4, 2023. https://theplanets.org/the-sun/

Patowary, Kaushik. "Alaska's Giant Vegetables." Amusing Planet. https://www.amusingplanet.com/2015/10/alaskas-giant-vegetables.html

Wilson, Tracy V., and Chris Pollette. "How Magnets Work." How Stuff Works. September 20, 2022. https://science.howstuffworks.com/magnet.htm

"Tracking How Magnetism Affects Animal Behavior." Science Daily. February 23, 2023. https://www.sciencedaily.com/releases/2023/02/230223132931.htm

Osborne, Margaret. "This Highschooler Invented a Low-Cost, Mind-Controlled Prosthetic Arm." Smithsonian Magazine. May 2, 2022. https://www.smithsonianmag.com/innovation/this-high-schooler-invented-a-low-cost-mind-controlled-prosthetic-arm-180979984/

"Our Story." Accessed June 4, 2023. https:// Ecovative.com

Rosen, Ellen. "Are Mushrooms the Future of Alternative Leather." *The New York Times*. December 25, 2022. https://www.nytimes.com/2022/12/14/business/leather-fake-mycelium-mushrooms-fashion.html

Canadian Association of Optometrists. "Fun Eye Facts." April 12, 2023. https://opto.ca/eye-health-library/fun-eye-facts.

Obed, Debra. "How many eyes do dragonflies have?" Creature Facts. July 7, 2022. https://creaturefacts.com/how-many-eyes-do-dragonflies-have/

Hall, Heather. "These 14 Animals Have the Largest Eyes in the World." AZ Animals. Updated April 14, 2023. https://a-z-animals.com/blog/these-14-animals-have-the-largest-eyes-in-the-world/

Daly, Ciaran. "Robocop Bot to Patrol Singapore and Stop Bad Behaviour Like Smoking and Illegal Parking. *Daily Star. September 6, 2021.* https://www.dailystar.co.uk/tech/robocop-bot-patrol-singapore-stop-24919093

Julia, Nina. "Diabetes Statistics: Facts & Latest Data in the US (2023 Update." CFAH. January 0, 2023. https:/cfah.org/diabetes-statistics/

"InnoMake – One Step Ahead." TechInno. Accessed June 4, 2023. https://www.tec-innovation.com/en/innomake.

Elizabeth Howell, and Daisy Dobrijevic. "James Webb Space Telescope (JWST), A Complete Guide." Space.com. April 27,2023. https://www.space.com/21925-james-webb-space-telescope-jwst.html

"The basics of microchips," ASML. Accessed June 4, 2023. https://www.asml.com/en/technology/all-about-microchips/microchip-basics

"Microchipping FAQ," AVMA. Accessed June 4, 2023. https://www.avma.org/resources-tools/pet-owners/petcare/microchips-reunite-pets-families/microchipping-faq

"21 Weird and Wonderful Facts About Scent and Smell." Park Candles. Accessed June 4, 2023. https://www.parkscandles.com/blog/21-weird-and-wonderful-facts-about-scents-and-smell/

"Training Dogs to Sniff Out COVID-19." Accessed June 4, 2023. https://pennovation.upenn.edu/news/gallery/training-dogs-sniff-out-covid-19

Mwamba, Seneo and Khanyi Mlaba. "12 Plastic Pollution Facts that Show Why We Need to Do More." Global Citizen. July 16, 2021. https://www.globalcitizen.org/en/content/effects-of-plastic-pollution-facts-you-should-know/

Printed in the United States
by Baker & Taylor Publisher Services